10/06

The Biography of Sugar

Rachel Eagen

Crabtree Publishing Company
www.crabtreebooks.com

Crabtree Publishing Company

www.crabtreebooks.com

For my brother, Nathan.

Coordinating editor: Ellen Rodger
Project editor: Carrie Gleason
Editors: Adrianna Morganelli, Michelle Nielsen
Production coordinator: Rosie Gowsell
Production assistance: Samara Parent
Art director: Rob MacGregor
Photo research: Allison Napier

Consultant: Wendy A. Woloson, Curator of Printed Books, Library Company of Philadelphia

Photo Credits: AP/ AP Wide World Photos: p. 26; The Art Archive/ Musée des Arts Africains et Océaniens/ Dagli Orti: p. 14; Bildarchiv Preussischer Kulturbesitz/ Art Resource, NY: p. 4; Biblioteca Estense, Modena, Italy, Giraudon/ Bridgeman Art Library: p. 10, p. 11 (bottom); Biblioteca Nacional Rio de Janeiro, Brazil/ Bridgeman Art Library: p. 17 (top); Bibliotheque Nationale, Paris, France, Lauros, Giraudon/ Bridgeman Art Library: p. 16; Private Collection, Archives Charmet/ Bridgeman Art Library: p. 28 (bottom); Private Collection/ Bridgeman Art Library: pp. 12-13, p. 18; Wilberforce House, Hull City Museums and Art Galleries, UK/ Bridgeman Art Library: p. 15 (bottom); Tony Arruza/ Corbis: p. 24 (top), p. 27 (middle right and bottom left); Bettmann/ Corbis: p. 19 (top), p. 21 (top); Corbis: p. 19 (bottom); Owen Franken/ Corbis: p. 9 (bottom); Phillip Gould/ Corbis: p. 5 (top), p. 27 (middle left); Richard Hamilton Smith/ Corbis: p. 9 (top); Historical Picture Archive/ Corbis: p. 11 (top); Jeremy Horner/ Corbis: p. 7 (top); Hulton-Deutsch Collection/ Corbis: p. 20; Lake County Museum/ Corbis: p. 21 (bottom), p. 30 (top); Les Stone/ Corbis: p. 22; Gideon Mendel/ Corbis: p. 24 (bottom); Richard T. Nowitz/ Corbis: p. 7 (bottom); Charles O'Rear/ Corbis: p. 31 (top); Carl & Ann Purcell/ Corbis: p. 25; Adam Woolfitt/ Corbis: p. 15 (top); Tony Clark/ The Image Works: cover; istock International: p. 27 (top right), p. 29, p. 30 (bottom); North Wind Picture Archives: p. 13 (top); Paul Smith/ Panos Pictures: p. 23 (bottom); Philip Wolmuth/ Panos Pictures: p. 23 (top); Joyce Photographics/ Photo Researchers, Inc.: p. 3, cover background; USDA/ Photo Researchers, Inc.: p. 31 (bottom); Other images from stock photo cd

Cartography: Jim Chernishenko: p. 8

Illustrations: Barbara Bedell: p. 6

Cover: Sucking on a piece of raw sugar makes a tasty treat.

Title page: Sugar is found in most products we eat everyday and in treats such as ice cream and jellybeans.

Contents: Sugar cane plants store sugar for energy in the stalks.

Crabtree Publishing Company

www.crabtreebooks.com   1-800-387-7650

Copyright © 2006 CRABTREE PUBLISHING COMPANY.
All rights reserved. No part of this publication may be reproduced, stored in a retrieval system or be transmitted in any form or by any means, electronic, mechanical, photocopying, recording, or otherwise, without the prior written permission of Crabtree Publishing Company. In Canada: We acknowledge the financial support of the Government of Canada through the Book Publishing Industry Development Program (BPIDP) for our publishing activities.

Cataloging-in-Publication Data
Eagen, Rachel, 1979-
    The biography of sugar / written by Rachel Eagen.
        p. cm. -- (How did that get here?)
    ISBN-13: 978-0-7787-2485-8 (rlb)
    ISBN-10: 0-7787-2485-9 (rlb)
    ISBN-13: 978-0-7787-2521-3 (pb)
    ISBN-10: 0-7787-2521-9 (pb)
1. Sugar cane--Juvenile literature. 2. Sugar beet--Juvenile literature. 3. Sugar--Juvenile literature. I. Title. II. Series.
    SB231.E24 2005
    633.6--dc22   2005019024
                                                          LC

Published in
the United States
PMB 16A
350 Fifth Ave.
Suite 3308
New York, NY
10118

Published
in Canada
616 Welland Ave.
St. Catharines
Ontario, Canada
L2M 5V6

Published in the
United Kingdom
73 Lime Walk
Headington
Oxford
OX3 7AD
United Kingdom

Published
in Australia
386 Mt. Alexander Rd.
Ascot Vale (Melbourne)
VIC 3032

Contents

A Sweet Commodity

Sugar is a common sweetener that is added to many foods available at the supermarket. It is used to sweeten drinks, to make desserts and candy, and as a **preservative** in jams and jellies. Sugar is also found in products that are not eaten, such as paints, plastics, and medicines.

Sugar Source

The sugar we use today comes from two different plants, sugar cane and sugar beets. There is no difference in the taste of sugar that comes from cane or beets, but the two plants are grown and **processed** differently. Sugar cane is a delicate plant that grows only in **tropical** climates, while sugar beets are a hardier crop that grow in the **temperate** climates of Europe and North America.

(right) In the 1700s, sugar became a valuable commodity in Europe. Sugar was enjoyed only by the rich, because governments charged a high tax to have it imported, or brought in from another country.

A Worldly Commodity

Today, sugar is widely available and is found in food products such as ketchup, hot chocolate, soda, cakes, pies, and candy bars. At one time, sugar was only grown in the tropical regions of the world, and was shipped great distances. For thousands of years, sugar has remained an important commodity, or good that can be bought and sold. Through wars, trade, and the enslavement of people, sugar is now grown, processed, and sold all over the world.

▲ *In 1841, sugar cubes were invented in what is now the Czech Republic. The operator of a sugar factory came up with the idea of making small sugar cubes after his wife cut her hand trying to cut a large lump of sugar into pieces.*

(above) Raw sugar is processed and made into white table sugar in a factory called a refinery. At this large refinery in the United States, a power shovel scoops up raw sugar.

What is Sugar?

Refined sugar is the white sugar crystals that we use at home. These sugar crystals are made from a sticky sap that plants produce. The scientific name for sugar is sucrose.

How Plants Make Sugar

All plants make sugar, or sucrose, through a process called photosynthesis. Plants make sugar for food. In photosynthesis, plants take in energy from the sun's rays through a green **pigment** in their leaves called chlorophyll.

The leaves also absorb carbon dioxide, a gas in the air that humans and animals breathe out. The combination of sunlight, carbon dioxide, and water, which plants absorb through their leaves and roots, allows photosynthesis to take place. Photosynthesis produces sucrose. Sucrose is carried to other parts of the plant, such as the leaves, stems, fruits, and roots, where it is stored as food. Some plants produce more sugar than others. Sugar cane and sugar beets are the two plants that produce the most sugar.

Photosynthesis

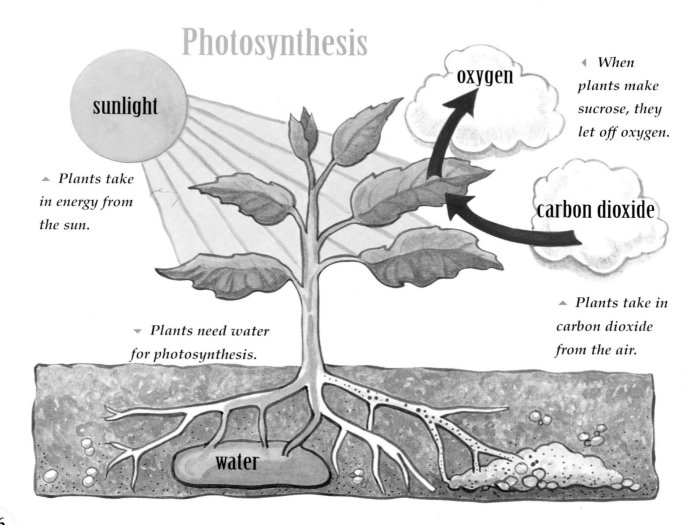

sunlight

oxygen

carbon dioxide

◄ When plants make sucrose, they let off oxygen.

▲ Plants take in energy from the sun.

▲ Plants take in carbon dioxide from the air.

▼ Plants need water for photosynthesis.

water

Growing Sugar Cane

Sugar cane is a large, grassy plant. It has a tall, hard stem where sugar is stored. To plant new sugar cane, cuttings of harvested cane, called setts, are buried in the soil. With enough water, the setts take root and new stems grow. Sugar cane does not have to be planted every year. After harvest, some of the stems are left underground. The following year, the stems grow back. This is called a ratoon crop. Ratoon crops produce sugar for three or four years before new cane crops have to be planted.

Growing Sugar Beets

Sugar beets are root vegetables. The part of the plants that store sugar is beneath the ground. Sugar beets grow in two stages. In the first year, stores of sugar build up in the roots, causing the beets to swell in size. This is when beets are harvested for their sugar. If left in the fields to grow, the beets produce seeds and cannot be processed for sugar. From the seeds, new plants are grown.

(above) Sugar collects inside the sugar cane stalks, which are yellow and fibrous.

(below) A sugar beet farmer inspects the leaves for signs of plant diseases.

Sugar Lands

Sugar cane is a tropical grass, which means it only grows in the tropics, the warm areas of the world just north and south of the equator. Sugar beets are a temperate crop, which means they grow in the colder, northern areas of the world. Sugar beets are a hardier crop than sugar cane, and can survive cold winters.

The First Crops

Sugar cane first grew wild on the Pacific island of New Guinea. Scientists believe that ash left behind from ancient volcanic eruptions **enriched** New Guinea's soil with **nutrients**. The nutrients, combined with heavy rainfall from seasonal **monsoons**, allowed sugar cane to begin to grow.

Over many centuries, sugar cane began to be cultivated, or grown as a crop. Sugar cane spread to other tropical areas, such as India and China. The hot, humid weather and fertile soil of the tropics provide ideal conditions for growing sugar cane. Today, sugar cane is an important crop on many Caribbean islands, such as Cuba, Barbados, Jamaica, Puerto Rico, and Haiti. Other major world producers of sugar cane are Brazil, Australia, Pakistan, China, Japan, India, and South Africa. In the United States, sugar cane is grown in Louisiana, Florida, and Hawaii. Most sugar cane is grown on plantations, or large farms that grow one main crop. This is because growing and harvesting sugar cane requires a large number of workers.

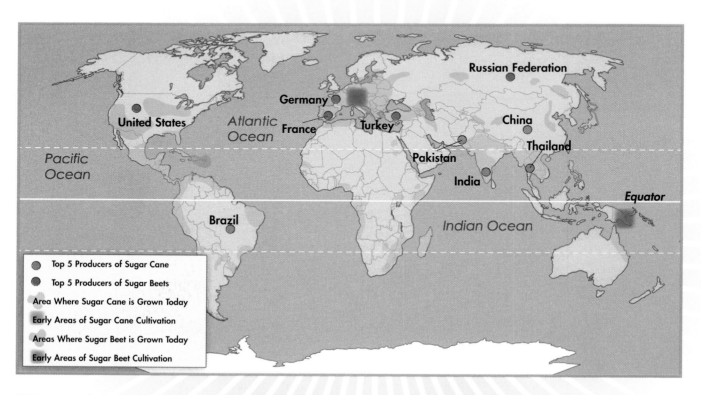

Russian Federation
Germany
United States
Atlantic Ocean
France
Turkey
China
Thailand
Pakistan
Pacific Ocean
India
Equator
Brazil
Indian Ocean

- Top 5 Producers of Sugar Cane
- Top 5 Producers of Sugar Beets
- Area Where Sugar Cane is Grown Today
- Early Areas of Sugar Cane Cultivation
- Areas Where Sugar Beet is Grown Today
- Early Areas of Sugar Beet Cultivation

This map shows where most of the world's sugar cane and sugar beets are grown today. It also shows where sugar cane and sugar beets originated.

Temperate Crops

Sugar beets were first found growing in Silesia, which is a region of Europe that includes parts of present-day Germany, Austria, Poland, and the Czech Republic. Today, sugar beets are grown and harvested in many countries, including the United States, Canada, England, Scotland, Sweden, Finland, France, Russia, and Germany. Sugar beets are often grown in rotation with other crops, which means that another crop, such as wheat, is grown on the same land in a different season. Crop rotation helps preserve the soil's nutrients, so that the land can be farmed from year to year without becoming **barren**. Sugar beets are usually grown on small farms.

A sugar beet absorbs about 13 gallons (50 L) of water during its first year of growth, making the root swell in size.

Sugar cane grows in some parts of southern China, where it is warm and wet. Here, sugar cane is being harvested by hand.

The Spread of Sugar

Thousands of years ago, the people of New Guinea harvested wild sugar cane and sucked and chewed on pieces of chopped sugar cane for energy. Ancient traders from Southeast Pacific islands journeyed by sea from island to island and to the mainland of Asia and eastern Africa to trade animals, metal tools, and food. Through trade, the cultivation of sugar cane spread.

Ancient India's Sugar

Refining sugar cane was first developed in India. In ancient India, sugar was called *gur*. *Gur* is a dark brown sugar made by crushing the cane in a press and boiling the juice. When the armies of Macedonian leader Alexander the Great reached India around 325 B.C., soldiers wrote reports of sugar. They described sugar as a reed, or tall grass, that made honey without needing bees. From India, the process of making sugar from sugar cane spread west to China and east to Persia, or present-day Iran. In Persia, irrigation, or watering, systems were built, which allowed sugar cane to be cultivated in the dry climate.

Islam and Sugar

In 632 A.D., **Arab Muslim** traders and **missionaries** traveled throughout Asia spreading their beliefs to other lands. They introduced sugar to areas within their trade routes around the Mediterranean, such as Syria, Cyprus, Egypt, Sicily, and Spain. Existing technologies from these areas, such as the edge-runner mill, a machine for crushing olives for oil and grapes for wine, were used to refine sugar.

Crusaders

In 1099, **Christian crusaders** invaded the Muslim controlled areas of Palestine and Syria. The crusaders brought the sugar back to northern European countries, such as England. Sugar was first used in northern Europe as medicine, and later as a sweetener in foods and drinks. Only kings, queens, and the very wealthy could afford to buy sugar. The method for extracting sugar from sugar beets, which grew in areas of northern Europe, had not yet been discovered.

(above) For centuries before sugar made its way around the world, honey, made by bees, was the main sweetener.

European Traders

By the late 1200s, traders from Venice, in what is now Italy, began to control the sugar trade. Spanish and Portuguese explorers used islands off the coast of Africa, such as Madeira, the Canary Islands, and São Tomé to grow sugar cane. Slaves captured from Africa were used to grow and harvest the cane for Europeans. By the 1470s, sugar refineries were built in the European cities of Venice, Bologna, and Antwerp to process sugar.

Discovering a New World

In 1492, explorer Christopher Columbus set sail for the New World, or what is now known as North, Central, and South America. Columbus claimed several Caribbean islands, or the West Indies, for Spain. In 1493, Columbus returned to the New World, this time with settlers, livestock such as cows and pigs, and plants for growing crops. Among the plants he brought to the West Indies, was sugar cane.

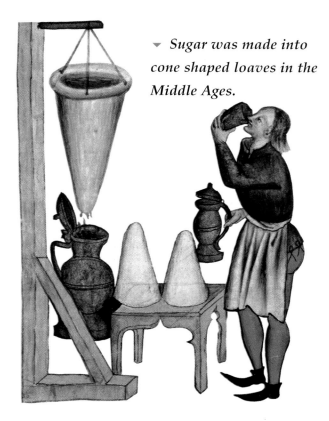

▼ *Sugar was made into cone shaped loaves in the Middle Ages.*

Refining Sugar the Old Way

To make sugar from cane, the sugar cane was crushed in a mill. Early mills were powered by humans or animals. Around 700 A.D., mills began to be powered by water wheels. After the mill, the crushed sugar cane was put into a press, which squeezed out more sugar juice. The juice was collected in buckets, and then boiled in copper pots. Boiling removed most of the water from the cane sap, but it was still full of **impurities**, such as dirt. Ashes were added to the boiled cane syrup, which caused most of the impurities to float to the surface as a layer of scum. The scum was scraped off the top of the mixture, and the sap was boiled again. This process was repeated until the cane syrup was clear. The sugar syrup was left to cool and then poured into clay pots and placed in a hot room. Within six days, the syrup in the pots turned into loaves of dry sugar, with a puddle of thick molasses at the bottom.

Caribbean Colonies

The 1400s to 1700s was a period of exploration and discovery for Europeans. While searching for new trade routes, explorers discovered new lands. European countries expanded their territories by building **colonies** in these lands. Colonies brought wealth to Europe in the form of natural resources and other products. The Spanish were the first to set up colonies on Caribbean islands. The Portuguese followed closely behind the Spanish and set up colonies in what is now the country of Brazil, on the South American mainland.

(below) Large sugar plantations required hundreds of workers to plant, harvest, and mill the sugar cane.

New World Sugar

Sugar cane cultivation spread to other Caribbean islands and South America by European colonists. In Brazil, Portuguese colonists owned large farming areas and rented, or leased, smaller sections to Portuguese planters to grow sugar cane. In return, planters paid the land owners with a percentage of their sugar cane crops. By 1550, Brazil had a large sugar shipment to export to Europe. Sugar cane plantations and mills were also set up on the Spanish controlled Caribbean islands, such as Hispaniola.

Vying for Control

The control of many Caribbean islands changed often during colonization. England, France, and the Netherlands joined Spain and Portugal as colonizers of the Caribbean and fought amongst themselves for the richest islands. On Barbados, English planters experimented with growing a variety of crops, such as tobacco and indigo, a plant that is used to make a blue dye, before turning to sugar cane. Sugar cane plantations were established in the 1640s, and Barbados quickly became the biggest producer of sugar in the Caribbean. Sugar plantations were built all over the Caribbean by Europeans eager to make money in the sugar trade.

Island Slaves

Sugar cane planting, harvesting, and milling required a large number of laborers. Early European colonists enslaved the Indians of the Caribbean and forced them to work on their farms and plantations. Overwork and diseases introduced by the colonists killed large numbers of Indians. In 1515, Spanish priest Bartolomé de Las Casas complained to the Spanish king that the Indians were being wiped out and suggested that slaves from Africa be brought to the West Indies to meet the demand for laborers. Las Casas later changed his mind about bringing slaves from Africa, but by that time, the tradition of African slavery in the New World had begun.

Triangular Trade

Captured Africans were bound with wooden shackles. A leather thong was tied around their necks, and attached to two other slaves. The long chain of people were marched to waiting slave ships.

The first African slaves to work on sugar plantations in the New World were brought to Brazil by the Portuguese in 1510. When other European countries began to set up sugar plantations in their colonies, the demand for slaves grew. In a system called the Triangular Trade, slave traders brought Africans from their villages to the West Indies and sold them into slavery. Slave traders brought valuable commodities from the New World, such as sugar and rum, back to Europe.

In Africa

Slave traders exchanged European goods, such as guns, for slaves on the West Coast of Africa. In Africa, slave ships docked in ports while slave raiders captured slaves inland and force-marched them to the coast. Many Africans died on this part of the journey. At slave ports, slaves were stripped naked for traders to examine them to make sure they were healthy enough for hard work, and could be sold for a high price in the West Indies.

The Middle Passage

Before leaving Africa, slaves were **branded** on the chest with hot irons to show who had purchased them. Slaves were considered the property of the traders. They were then chained in the hull, or body, of the ships for the journey across the Atlantic Ocean. The voyage across the Atlantic Ocean from West Africa to the West Indies was known as the Middle Passage. It took about five weeks for a slave ship to cross the Atlantic. During this time, slaves were not allowed up on deck, because some slaves would jump ship and drown themselves if they had the chance. Below deck, slaves were not allowed to wash, and they were packed so tightly together that they could barely move. Slaves often became ill from not having enough food or water. Many died before they reached the West Indies. On some ships, slaves revolted against the traders.

In the West Indies

In the West Indies, slaves were sold for five times the amount for which they had been bought in Africa. At slave auctions and markets, slaves were made to stand on a platform while plantation owners bid on them. Sometimes, entire boatloads of slaves were sold in bulk to a singe plantation owner. In other cases, slaves were separated from their families and sold to different plantations. Slaves from different parts of Africa did not speak the same language as each other or the language of their new owners.

Back to Europe

Slave traders used the money they made from selling slaves to buy large amounts of sugar, and products that are made from sugar, such as molasses and rum. With ships full of valuable cargo, the traders headed home to Europe, where they in turn sold the goods to merchants who then sold them to their customers. From start to finish, the journey from Europe to Africa, then from Africa to the West Indies, and back to Europe, usually took about one year.

◀ *Slaves were shackled with iron rings to prevent them from escaping.*

▼ *Almost 12 million Africans were taken from Africa to work as slaves from 1450 to the 1800s. Captured slaves were sold or rented to plantation owners at auctions.*

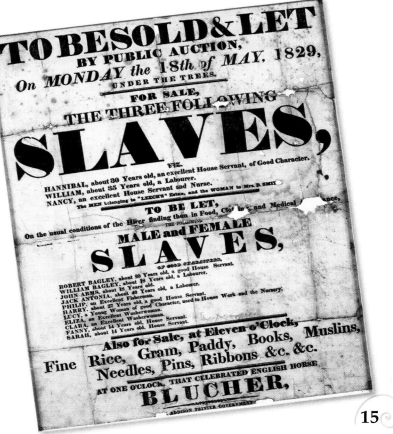

TO BE SOLD & LET
BY PUBLIC AUCTION,
On MONDAY the 18th of MAY, 1829,
UNDER THE TREES.
FOR SALE,
THE THREE FOLLOWING
SLAVES,
VIZ.
HANNIBAL, about 30 Years old, an excellent House Servant, of Good Character.
WILLIAM, about 35 Years old, a Labourer.
NANCY, an excellent House Servant and Nurse.
The MEN belonging to "LEECK'S" Estate, and the WOMAN to Mrs. D. SMIT.

TO BE LET,
On the usual conditions of the Hirer finding them in Food, Clothes, and Medical Attendance,
THE FOLLOWING
MALE and FEMALE
SLAVES,
ROBERT BAGLEY, about 20 Years old, a good House Servant.
WILLIAM BAGLEY, about 18 Years old, a Labourer.
JOHN ARMS, about 18 Years old.
JACK ANTONIA, about 40 Years old, a Labourer.
HARRY, an Excellent Fisherman.
HARRY, about 27 Years old, a good House Servant, used to House Work and the Nursery.
LUCY, a Young Woman of good Character.
ELIZA, an Excellent Washerwoman.
CLARA, about 14 Years old, House Servant.
FANNY, about 14 Years old, House Servant.
SARAH, about 14 Years old, House Servant.

Also for Sale, at Eleven o'Clock,
Fine Rice, Gram, Paddy, Books, Muslins,
Needles, Pins, Ribbons &c. &c.
AT ONE O'CLOCK, THAT CELEBRATED ENGLISH HORSE
BLUCHER,
ADDISON PRINTER GOVERNMENT

Sugar Cane Plantations

Sugar plantations in the New World were established on the islands of the Caribbean, in South America, and in what is now the southern United States. Slave labor was used on all sugar cane plantations.

Plantation Owners

The owners of some Caribbean sugar plantations were Europeans who rarely visited their plantations. They remained in Europe but collected money made from the sale of sugar. Other plantations were run by their owners. At one time, so much money could be made from owning a sugar plantation that sugar was called "white gold." Plantation owners and **overseers** lived with their families in large, beautiful homes. Some of their slaves worked as maids, butlers, cooks, and coachmen in the homes.

Daily Life of a Slave

Slaves worked Monday to Saturday, from dawn to dusk. They were given only two or three short breaks during the day for food and water. Slaves were often not fed enough and many became ill. Slaves built their own small homes from wattle, or woven branches, which were plastered and topped with palm thatched roofs. They had no personal possessions and slept on the ground or on beds of straw. Outside their homes they grew vegetable gardens, which they tended after long days of work in sugar cane fields.

(below) Slaves not only worked in the fields planting and harvesting sugar cane, but also in mills and refineries. At mills, they labored under the hot sun boiling the sugar cane juice to make raw sugar.

Work and Punishment

Plantation work was organized so that the strongest and healthiest men and women did most of the physical work. In the fall, slaves planted the cane in trenches dug with hoes. Slaves kept fields clear of weeds until the sugar cane was ready to be harvested. Child slaves weeded and collected the green fodder, or leaves and stalks, that was fed to livestock. At harvest time, slaves cut the sugar cane, operated the mills, and made the dry sugar. Work in the mills was not only hot, it was also dangerous. Some slaves lost their arms in the rollers that fed the cane into the crushing mill. Slaves were flogged, or whipped, by overseers so that they continued to work at a fast pace, even when they were exhausted.

(right) Slaves who misbehaved or who were thought to be lazy were beaten.

Anansi Stories

Slaves on sugar plantations in the West Indies entertained each other with folktales about a black spider named Anansi. In the stories, Anansi faced struggles with larger animals, such as rats, pigs, and sheep, but Anansi always outsmarted them in the end. Anansi stories originally came from Ghana, Africa.

Historians believe slaves in the West Indies adapted the stories so that Anansi represented themselves, while the larger animals represented the plantation owners. It is thought that slaves told each other Anansi stories to provide comfort from the pains of their daily lives on the plantations. Anansi stories are still told in the Caribbean, even though slavery has ended.

Slave Revolt

Some slaves on sugar cane plantations organized uprisings against their owners. Rebel slaves risked hanging if they did not succeed.

The Haitian Revolution

In 1791, Saint Dominigue was a French colony on the island of Hispaniola. Slaves in the colony produced more sugar than anywhere else in the West Indies. When the French government promised people who were of mixed race their rights, such as allowing them to vote, white planters became angry. At the time, the British had lost their colonies in the United States and were eager to gain some of the wealth that a takeover of Saint Dominigue provided.

The white planters made a deal with the British to take over the island. Slaves joined free people of mixed race and rose up against the colonizers in the largest slave revolt in history, called the Haitian Revolution. They burned the sugar plantations and killed many planters. After 13 years of fighting, the slaves succeeded in creating the first free black **republic**, which today is called Haiti. The fight of slaves for freedom in Haiti sparked the liberation of other slaves all over the West Indies. Slaves in Venezuela, on the South American mainland, planned their own successful revolt against their owners with help from the free Haitians, who supplied guns and troops.

Toussaint L'Ouverture

Toussaint L'Ouverture was a black slave who worked on a sugar plantation in Saint Dominigue. He was taught to read and write and was trusted by his plantation owner to oversee other slaves. When the Haitian Revolution broke out, Toussaint L'Ouverture recruited his own army of slaves. In 1798, Toussaint became the ruler of the island. The French government, under the leadership of General Napoleon Bonaparte, sent soldiers to capture Toussaint L'Ouverture and reclaim the island. Toussaint L'Ouverture died in a French prison in 1803, but is today remembered as a hero of the Haitian Revolution.

Many people lost their lives in their fight for freedom from slavery.

Abolitionists

Slaves were not the only ones who opposed slavery. From the late 1700s, **abolitionists** in England and the United States pressured their governments to end slavery. The abolitionists believed that slaves should be treated as human beings and not as property. Slavery was abolished in the British colonies of the West Indies in 1834, but continued in a different form as former slaves were paid so little that they continued to live in slave-like conditions. The official end of slavery in the West Indies was on August 1, 1838.

A New Kind of Slavery

The end of slavery on sugar plantations caused plantation owners to lose profits, because they had to pay people to work. Plantation owners looked to the Far East to solve this problem. From 1800 to 1847, laborers from China and Japan came to plantations on the present-day islands of Cuba, Jamaica, and Hawaii. The workers were paid very little for their work.

▼ *Asian workers on Caribbean sugar plantations signed a contract with the plantation owners, which did not allow them to leave the plantations.*

19

Europe's Sugar Beets

Once used as a rare treat, sugar developed into an invaluable commodity in Europe by the late 1700s. It was combined with cocoa, another commodity that was growing in popularity, to make chocolate. Coffee and tea, which were introduced to Europe in the 1600s, were becoming popular as well. Sugar was needed to sweeten these bitter drinks.

West Indies Sugar Decline

With the end of slavery in the West Indies, plantation owners in some places were forced to pay their workers. Banks failed as planters no longer had the money to repay loans and plantation estates were abandoned or sold. The result was a drop in sugar production in the West Indies. At the same time, abolitionists in Europe and North America were boycotting, or refusing to buy, West Indies sugar because slave-like conditions still existed on some plantations.

Napoleon's Sugar

In the early 1800s, Britain and France went to war against each other in what was called the Napoleonic Wars. During the war, British ships blocked French trading ports, cutting off France's imports of sugar from the West Indies. France had also lost control of Saint Dominigue, later called Haiti, and faced a sugar shortage. By this time, the French already knew how to make sugar from sugar beets, thanks to the work of Olivier de Serres in 1575. To combat the sugar shortage, the French leader Napoleon ordered that sugar be made from sugar beets. Sugar beets grew easily in the temperate climate of France. Many farmers were already growing sugar beets as a rotation crop, so processing and refining sugar from the beets came as an added boost to French farmers' incomes.

▶ *Women workers put sugar icing on cookies at a factory in Europe in the 1920s. By growing sugar beets in Europe, sugar products became more readily available.*

Sugar Beet Factories

By 1813, France had 334 factories that produced sugar from sugar beets. Other countries with similar climates, such as Germany and Russia, also began growing and processing sugar beets. European countries that grew and processed their own sugar beets were no longer dependent on sugar from colonies in the West Indies.

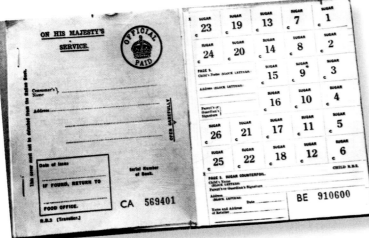

World Wars

For most of Europe, sugar beets became the main source of sugar. England still received its sugar from its colonies, especially Jamaica. When **World War I** broke out in 1914, Britain realized how much it depended on its colonies for sugar when German submarines blocked ports and stopped sugar from reaching England. After the war, Britain began to grow sugar beets and refine sugar on its own soil. In the United States, the government encouraged farmers to grow sugar beets to supply its citizens with sugar. By the 1940s, sugar-beet production was starting to succeed in the United States Midwest.

◄ *In England during World War II, sugar was in short supply. Citizens received ration books, which allowed them eight ounces (227 g) of sugar per person each week.*

(above) In this Kansas postcard from around 1905, farmers are shown working in a sugar beet field. Large sugar refining companies were established in the United States to process beet sugar.

Sugar Cane Workers Today

Sugar cane plantations still operate today in tropical countries. Sugar cane cultivation is mostly done by hand and continues to require many workers. In most cases, workers on sugar cane plantations are paid low wages and work under poor conditions. On the Caribbean island of Cuba, sugar accounts for up to 70 percent of the country's revenue, or income. Belize, the Dominican Republic, and Haiti are also important sugar producers.

Haitian Sugar

Many Haitians leave their homes to work seasonally in the sugar cane fields of the nearby country of Dominican Republic. There are not enough jobs for people in Haiti, so they are forced to leave their country to find work. In the Dominican Republic, Haitian sugar cane workers must pay to have a physical exam to make sure they are strong enough to work.

Sugar cane workers also have to pay for their own food and shelter on the plantations. Many sugar cane workers struggle with debt even though they come to the Dominican plantations to make enough money to support themselves and their families back in Haiti.

Bateyes

Sugar cane workers in the Dominican Republic build their own villages, called *bateyes*, on the plantations. The narrow, long buildings are divided into small windowless rooms where up to four workers live together. The workers often have to sleep on beds without mattresses.

▶ *After the Haitian Revolution, Haitians were left to manage the devastated plantations. Agriculture in Haiti never fully recovered, and today the country is one of the poorest in the world.*

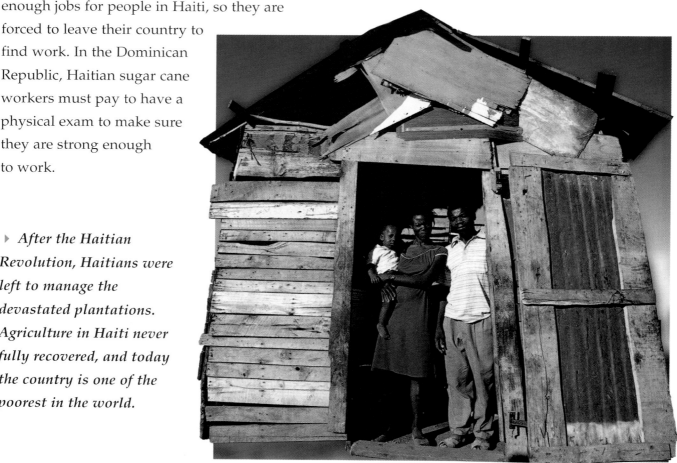

Plantation Workers

Human rights organizations report that Haitian plantation workers are not paid regularly, and may go without pay for several months. Wages are as low as five dollars a day. Haitian workers who wish to leave the sugar cane plantation to work elsewhere can be arrested as **illegal immigrants**, as their work permits cannot be used in any other part of the country. Workers who leave the plantation can be arrested and sent to jail. Many jails in the Dominican Republic force their prisoners to work on sugar cane plantations as part of their punishment.

Recruiting Workers

Some sugar cane workers are recruited for work in the Dominican Republic by *buscones*. *Buscones* are people paid by plantation owners to find Haitians who will work on sugar plantations. *Buscones* promise Haitians money, good living conditions, and easy work on the plantations. Once the workers get to the plantations, they find that these promises are not met but they cannot afford to return home.

(above) On sugar cane plantations, workers bend and stretch in the tropical sun for nine to 12 hours at a time to harvest the cane.

Child Workers

In some countries, such as the Philippines and El Salvador, children, sometimes as young as eight years old, work in sugar cane fields. Aside from the difficulty of the work, children often hurt themselves using harvesting equipment, such as large knives called machetes. These children are forced to miss several months of school during the harvest, which causes them to fall behind in their studies. Often, the families of the children live in poverty and the children work to help support the family.

Harvesting Sugar

Harvesting sugar cane requires a lot of work, especially in countries where the crop is harvested by hand using machetes. Most plantations have sugar mills close to the cane fields so that the sugar can be processed right away. This is important because if left exposed to air, cane sap spoils about one day after the sugar cane is cut.

Machines, such as this combine, are used in some countries to harvest sugar cane.

Beet Machines

Machines are used to harvest sugar beets. A machine moves down the rows of sugar beets, and cuts off the leafy crowns, then another machine follows behind and pulls the beets from the soil. The sugar inside a sugar beet lasts several months before it spoils, so it is not necessary to process the beets as soon as they are harvested.

Burning the Sugar Cane

One way of harvesting sugar is to set fire to the cane fields. Sugar cane has a tough husk, or outer covering, so burning cane stalks does not damage the sugar inside. After the fields have been burned, people gather the stalks. This practice is easier than chopping the cane down by hand, and it is useful for ridding the fields of pests, such as insects and rats. Cane burning is not allowed in most parts of the world, because it releases many harmful toxins, or dangerous chemicals, into the air.

At the Sugar Mill

After harvesting, sugar cane is taken from the fields to a nearby mill. At the sugar mill, the cane is fed into machines that chop it into little pieces. These pieces are then pressed to extract some of the sugar juice. The pieces pass through a diffuser, where powerful jets of hot water rinse the sugar juice from the cane.

Cleaning the Sugar

The dark and cloudy sugar juice is **purified** before it can be turned into sugar crystals. In tanks called clarifiers, a chemical called lime is added to the sugar juice. Lime causes impurities, such as dirt, to rise to the surface in a layer of scum. The scum is scraped away, and the purer sugar solution is moved to a set of boilers called evaporators. The evaporators boil the sugar until most of the water is removed. A thick, sticky sugar syrup remains.

Seeding and Spinning

A small amount of refined sugar crystals are added to the sugar syrup. This is called seeding the sugar, and it helps the sugar in the syrup to crystallize. The sugar is spun in a large metal drum called a **centrifuge**. Crystals of sugar collect on the sides of the drum, and the remaining sap is drained and stored so it can be used later to make other products. The sugar crystals that come from the centrifuge are covered in a thin layer of molasses. These crystals are called raw sugar.

(above) At a sugar mill in Colombia, two men stir raw, milled sugar from sugar cane. Raw sugar is shipped to refineries for further processing.

Refining Sugar

Raw sugar is sent from the sugar cane mill to a refinery. Raw sugar is yellow to brown in color, and is much more coarse than table sugar. The thin layer of molasses that covers raw sugar protects the sugar crystals during shipping. At the refinery, raw sugar is made into different types of sugar that are packaged and sold in supermarkets or shipped to factories that make sweet products.

▼ *Large sugar refineries, such as this one in Montana, U.S.A., process sugar beets into sugar crystals.*

Sticky Molasses

Molasses is pure sugar juice that is squeezed directly from sugar cane or sugar beets. It is an extremely sweet syrup. Molasses that is drained from boiled sugar juice is called first molasses. Molasses increases in thickness and decreases in sweetness as sugar is processed into crystals. Backstrap molasses is thick and bitter. It forms at the last stage of crystallization and is used to make taffy and other sweets.

FACTORY PILER # 3

At the Beet Factory

Sugar beets are sent to refineries for processing. Sugar beets do not spoil as easily as sugar cane sap does, so the beets can be stored without spoiling. In the refinery, sugar beets go through several stages to be made into sugar.

▲ *Step 1: Sugar beets are washed and thinly sliced by machines. Sliced pieces of beet are called cossettes. Cossettes are put into a diffuser, which uses hot water to extract the sugar juice from inside the beets.*

▲ *Step 2: The raw sugar juice is mixed with a chemical called lime and a gas called carbon dioxide in carbonation tanks. This step removes impurities from the raw juice.*

▷ *Step 3: Inside a vacuum pan, the water from the juice evaporates, or turns into a gas. As the water is removed, sugar crystals begin to form and the mixture becomes a thick syrup.*

▲ *Step 4: In a centrifuge, the syrupy mixture is spun at a high speed to remove the remaining water and allow sugar crystals to fully form.*

▷ *Step 5: The sugar crystals are washed, dried, and packaged in bags for shipment to stores.*

Sugar Uses

Sugar is used to make delicious foods, such as cookies, chocolate, and other candy. Sugar is added to most processed foods, such as bread, not only to make it taste better, but because it is an excellent preservative. Sugar works with the juices in fruit to help preserve jams and jellies. Sugar also lowers the temperature at which foods freeze, which is one reason it is added to ice cream. Soft drinks and many fruit juices are made almost entirely from sugar.

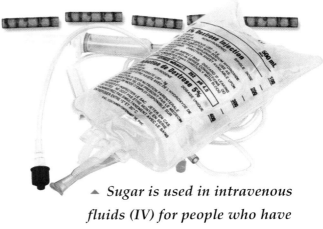

▲ *Sugar is used in intravenous fluids (IV) for people who have had surgery in hospitals.*

Sugar in Medicine

Sugar has become an important product in the medical field. Sugar is a source of energy that is quickly absorbed by the human body. Sugar tablets are included in emergency survival kits prepared by most militaries. Sugar placebos are sugar pills that doctors give to patients.

Placebos contain no real medicine, but patients believe they are getting better because of the pills. Scientists use sugar to grow **antibiotic** medicines to treat illnesses and infections. Dextran is a sticky by-product made when sugar is processed. When doctors do not have blood to give patients who need blood transfusions, a weak solution of dextran is used.

LA PREMIÈRE CURE.

Tiens Bichette une joutte de Rhum ; rien d'excellent comme ça pour la migraine

Molasses to Rum

Rum is a strong alcoholic drink made from molasses. Rum is made cheaply from the leftover sugar sludge that is produced during sugar processing. Rum does not spoil easily. From 1655 until the 1970s, sailors in the British navy were given a ration of rum each day. During the 1700s, molasses was shipped to New England colonies and made into rum. New England rum was traded by settlers in North America to native peoples for animal furs.

During a movement called temperance in the 1800s, cartoons warned people of the dangers of consuming rum. One of the goals of temperance was to get people to consume less alcohol.

Types of Sugar

Brown sugar is made by adding a bit of molasses back into raw sugar. Brown sugar is very sticky and heavy. It is usually used in baking.

Granulated sugar is the type found in most kitchens. Sugar cubes are lumps of sugar glued into cubes using a sugar syrup.

Sugar syrup is sugar in its liquid form. It is specially processed to prevent sugar crystals from forming. Golden syrup is a sugar syrup.

Every Last Bit...

Crushed sugar cane and beets that have been squeezed dry at the factory are shipped to other factories to be made into cattle feed. Dry canes and cossettes, or sliced sugar beets, can also be made into a pulp that is used to make newsprint. The fibrous canes and cossettes may be turned into nylon or types of plastic, which are used in many industries worldwide, including the clothing industry.

The leftover sugar juice that is not made into crystals also has many uses. Sugar water is mixed with molasses to make fertilizer, which helps to keep soil healthy. It can be recycled and used for fuel to move the turbines in the sugar factory. In Brazil, sugar cane is made into a fuel called ethanol to power cars.

▼ *New automobiles known as flex fuel cars, can run on fuel made from sugar.*

The Future of Sugar

People like sugar for its sweet taste, but some people avoid it because eating too much sugar has been associated with health problems, such as tooth decay and **obesity**. Scientists have been working on sugar alternatives, or substitutes, for over a hundred years, but some of them are thought to cause more serious illnesses, such as cancer. In some countries, certain sugar substitutes are banned because of health concerns. Several sugar substitutes have become popular among health-conscious people who are trying to cut sugar out of their diets. As food companies continue to add sugar and sugar syrup to processed foods, consumers, often unknowingly, are consuming more sugar than ever before.

(right) Many advertisements for foods that are high in sugar, such as ice cream, are targeted at children. Some scientists believe that too much sugar may cause health problems later in life.

SUNSHINE DAIRY ICE CREAM CONES

Gee! Dad I'm Lucky

This card and 5 cents entitles me to an Extra Large 10 cent cone of Sunshine Dairy Ice Cream.

5A-H1047

The Alternatives

Sweetener
Sugar Substitute

Sugar substitutes are chemicals used to artificially sweeten food. Aspartame is one of the most famous sugar substitutes, and is used in diet sodas and some chewing gums today. Aspartame was developed by James Schlatter in 1965 while he was trying to develop medicines to help cure stomach ulcers. One of the newest sugar alternatives is called Splenda. Sugar substitutes are popular among people on diets because they have little or no **calories**.

Pollution

In the past, sugar mills and refineries dumped wastewater into lakes and streams. This water, used in the processing of sugar, has small amounts of sugar in it, and the sugar reduces the amount of oxygen in the water. Aquatic plants and fish breathe in oxygen from the water, so they can suffocate if there is not enough oxygen in the water. Most sugar refineries and mills have changed their practices so that the sugary wastewater is boiled and released into the air as steam, rather than into nearby streams.

Crop Diseases

Farmers face the danger of losing their sugar beet and sugar cane crops to plant diseases. Diseases such as white leaf, red stripe, yellow spot, and virus yellow can ruin sugar cane and sugar beet crops. Pests such as caterpillars, rats, and locusts also harm the plants by eating the leaves. Damaged crops leave farmers with nothing from which to cultivate the next year's crop. Pesticides are chemicals that farmers spray on the leaves of sugar cane and sugar beets to kill unwanted pests, but pesticides can also kill other plants and animals. Pesticides drain into nearby lakes and streams when heavy rains wash the chemicals off of the leaves. This pollutes the water, which can seriously harm or kill plants and animals, as well as people.

(left) A scientist in a field examines sugar beets for diseases.

Glossary

abolitionists People who fought to end slavery

antibiotic A medicine used to treat infections

Arab Muslim A follower of Islam and the teachings of the prophet Muhammad from Arabia, or present day Saudi Arabia

barren Empty of life or the ability to support it

brand To mark a person's flesh to show that they are the property of someone else

calories Units of energy

centrifuge A spinning machine that separates a substance into its different parts

Christian crusaders Followers of Jesus Christ who invaded the Holy Land, or present-day Palestine, during the Middle Ages

colony Land ruled by a distant country

enrich To improve soil by adding fertilizer

human rights organization A group of people who investigate and make others aware of the rights of people living in certain areas

illegal immigrants People who move to another country without that country's permission

impurities Substances that lower the quality of a product

missionaries People who go to another land to teach others about their religion

monsoons Seasonal winds of Southern Asia

nutrients Substances that help living things grow

obesity A medical condition describing a person who is extremely overweight

overseers Managers or supervisors in charge of other workers

pigment A substance that creates a specific color

preservative A substance that prevents food from rotting

processed A good that is manufactured, or changed from its original state

purify To remove impurities

refined The process of making a raw substance into a more pure product

republic A state or system of government where power rests with citizens who vote for their leaders

temperate A climate that experiences a range of seasons, such as summer and winter

tropical Regions of the world just north and south of the equator

vacuum pan A device in which water is evaporated from a substance

World War I An international conflict that lasted from 1914 to 1918

Index

1 2 3 4 5 6 7 8 9 0 Printed in the U.S.A. 4 3 2 1 0 9 8 7 6 5